Mademoiselle **BERGERON**
and Mrs. **O'LEARY**
demonstrate their
favorite Contortions

The magnificent
HORACE BARRÉ,
one of Quebec's most celebrated strongmen

James **CORBETT**,
the famous Boxer

Watch **BERGERON**
bend Iron Nails and
Silver Coins with his Teeth!

THE STRONGEST MAN IN THE WORLD

LOUIS CYR

NICOLAS DEBON

GROUNDWOOD BOOKS
HOUSE OF ANANSI PRESS
TORONTO BERKELEY

Groundwood Books / House of Anansi Press
110 Spadina Avenue, Suite 801, Toronto, Ontario M5V 2K4
Distributed in the USA by Publishers Group West
1700 Fourth Street, Berkeley, CA 94710

We acknowledge for their financial support of our publishing
program the Canada Council for the Arts, the Government of Canada
through the Book Publishing Industry Development Program (BPIDP)
and the Ontario Arts Council.

ONTARIO ARTS COUNCIL
CONSEIL DES ARTS DE L'ONTARIO

Library and Archives Canada Cataloging in Publication
Debon, Nicolas
The strongest man in the world: Louis Cyr / Nicolas Debon.
ISBN-13: 978-0-88899-731-9
ISBN-10: 0-88899-731-0
1. Cyr, Louis, 1863-1912–Juvenile literature. 2. Strong men–Québec
(Province)–Biography–Juvenile literature. 3. Weight lifters–Québec
(Province)–Biography–Juvenile literature. I. Title.
CT9997.C97D42 2007   j796.41092   C2006-904934-3

Printed and bound in China

NEXT WAS AN IRISHMAN. HE WAS QUICK AND NERVOUS.

AT ONE POINT HE MANAGED TO RAISE ONE OF THE HORSE'S HOOVES.

ITS LEG MOVED! I'M THE WINNER!

YOU MOVED A HOOF, BUT YOU DIDN'T LIFT THE HORSE!

THEN IT WAS MY TURN. I WORE MY HAIR LONG BACK THEN. MY MOTHER USED TO CALL ME HER LITTLE SAMSON.

YOUNG MAN, WHY NOT TAKE OFF YOUR JACKET SO THE AUDIENCE CAN ADMIRE YOUR FINE PHYSIQUE?

NO, THANK YOU, SIR... I DON'T WANT TO SOIL MY NEW SHIRT.

I TOOK MORE TIME THAN THE OTHER COMPETITORS AS I SLID UNDER THE HORSE AND CAREFULLY POSITIONED MY HANDS AND FEET.

A FEW SECONDS LATER, I LIFTED ALL FOUR HOOVES OFF THE GROUND!

LADIES AND GENTLEMEN, THE... THE NEW **CHAMPION OF AMERICA!**

THE BIGGEST BOULDER HAD A QUESTION MARK PAINTED ON IT INSTEAD OF A NUMBER. IT WAS SO HEAVY IT HAD NOT EVEN BEEN WEIGHED.

INSTEAD OF TRYING TO LIFT THE 450-POUND ROCK, MICHAUD APPROACHED THE BIGGEST BOULDER.

HE KNEW THAT HIS TITLE DEPENDED ON THIS LIFT. BUT THE BOULDER WOULDN'T MOVE.

THEN IT WAS MY TURN... I WAS THINKING ABOUT GRANDPA CYR. HOW PROUD HE WOULD HAVE BEEN TO SEE ME THERE...

...AND MY DEAR MÉLINA... I DIDN'T WANT TO DISAPPOINT HER.

...AND SO, ONCE AGAIN, I WAS THE WINNER!

THE CONTEST WITH MICHAUD BROUGHT ME SOME FAME, BUT THE ONLY INCOME WE HAD CAME FROM THE SEASONAL JOBS I COULD FIND.

YOUR MOTHER GOT SICK, AND WE LOST OUR FIRST CHILD SHORTLY AFTER HER BIRTH.

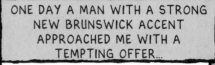

ONE DAY A MAN WITH A STRONG NEW BRUNSWICK ACCENT APPROACHED ME WITH A TEMPTING OFFER...

MR. CYR, MY NAME IS MACSOHMER. I'VE READ ABOUT YOUR EXPLOITS IN THE NEWSPAPERS...

...IF YOU TOUR THE COUNTRY FOR ME, I'LL MAKE YOU A WORLD-CLASS CELEBRITY!

I CAN OFFER YOU TWENTY-FIVE DOLLARS A WEEK!

MÉLINA! TWENTY-FIVE DOLLARS... THAT'S MORE THAN WE EVER...

MY HUSBAND WON'T WORK FOR LESS THAN FORTY!

AND SO WE AGREED ON THIRTY-FIVE DOLLARS A WEEK. IT WAS HARD WORK, BUT I SOON LEARNED THE SKILLS AND TRICKS OF A PROFESSIONAL SHOWMAN.

WHERE'S THE FRENCHMAN??! THE AUDIENCE IS ABOUT TO STORM THE STAGE!

UNFORTUNATELY, THINGS WENT WRONG VERY QUICKLY. ALL I GOT PAID AFTER WORKING FOR TWO MONTHS WAS...FIVE DOLLARS.

SIR, THE CYRS' ROOM IS EMPTY... AND ALL THEIR BELONGINGS HAVE DISAPPEARED, TOO!

ONE NIGHT, TIRED OF MACSOHMER'S LIES AND BRAGGING, WE DECIDED TO GO BACK HOME.

I PERFORMED IN BARNS AND HALLS ALL OVER THE COUNTRY. I LEARNED TO PREPARE MY ACTS WITH CARE, REHEARSING EVERY MOVEMENT OVER AND OVER AGAIN.

I WAS OFTEN CHALLENGED BY LOCAL BULLIES, AND I WOULD OFFER A LARGE SUM OF MONEY TO ANYONE ABLE TO LIFT MY WEIGHTS.

I SOON LEARNED TO KEEP A SCALE ON THE STAGE TO SETTLE ANY DISPUTES.

AS MY REPUTATION GREW, I BECAME MORE SUCCESSFUL. I BOUGHT A TAVERN WHERE PEOPLE COULD COME TO WATCH WEIGHTLIFTING AND OTHER ENTERTAINMENT.

YOU MAY BE TOO YOUNG TO REMEMBER, ÉMILIANA, BUT YOUR MOTHER AND I SPENT SOME HAPPY TIMES THERE!

I WAS ALSO FAMOUS FOR MY APPETITE. I COULD EAT MORE FOOD THAN FOUR PEOPLE AT ONE SITTING, WINNING ANY CONTEST IN GLUTTONY!

NO CHALLENGE SEEMED TOO DIFFICULT. I EXPENDED MY ENERGY WITH NO RESTRAINT.

MY STRENGTH SEEMED BOUNDLESS. I HAD THE STRANGE SENSATION THAT I WAS INVINCIBLE.

MY MOTHER WAS RIGHT TO CALL ME SAMSON. IT WAS AS THOUGH I WAS A REINCARNATION OF THE BIBLICAL HERO.

ONE OF MY MOST FAMOUS FEATS DATES BACK TO THOSE DAYS. IN 1891, IN MONTRÉAL, I RESISTED THE PULL OF FOUR HORSES WEIGHING 1,200 POUNDS EACH...

THE FOLLOWING YEAR, I WAS INVITED ON A TOUR OF EUROPE, WHERE STRONGMEN WERE HELD IN HIGH ESTEEM.

IN ENGLAND, I WAS GREETED BY CROWDS OF JOURNALISTS WHO HAD HEARD OF MY EXPLOITS.

HEIGHT: 5 FEET, 11 INCHES; WEIGHT: 320 POUNDS...

WITH MY HAIR FRESHLY CUT AND GROOMED LIKE A POODLE, I WAS A CURIOSITY TO THE PEOPLE OVER THERE!

BICEPS: 24 INCHES; NECK: 22 INCHES; FOREARMS: 19 INCHES...

...CHEST: 60 INCHES; THIGHS: 36 INCHES; CALVES... 28 INCHES!

MY FIRST PERFORMANCE IN LONDON WAS COMPLETELY SOLD OUT. FIVE THOUSAND PEOPLE WERE TURNED AWAY AT THE GATES.

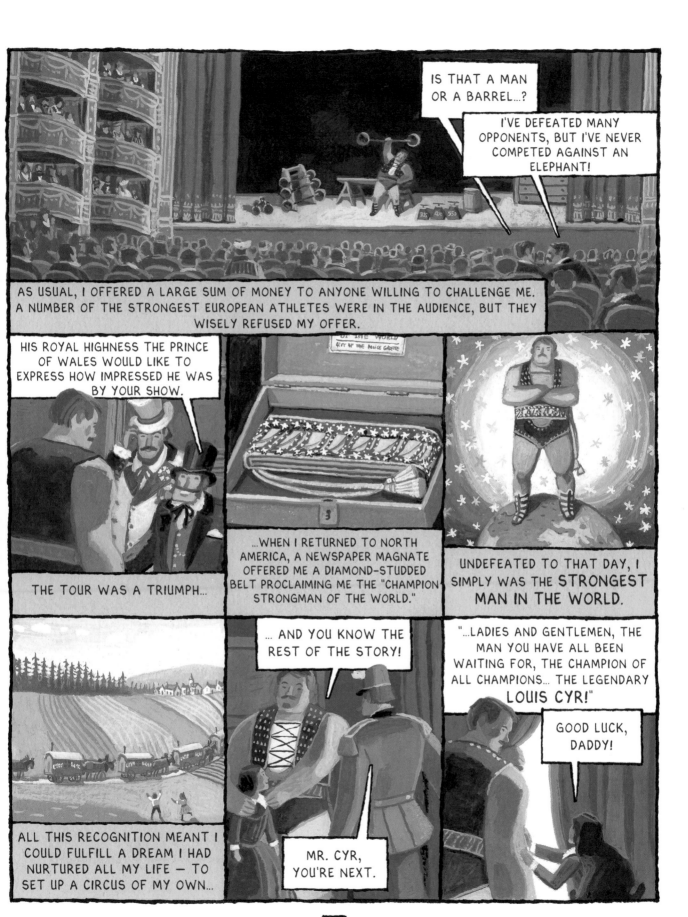

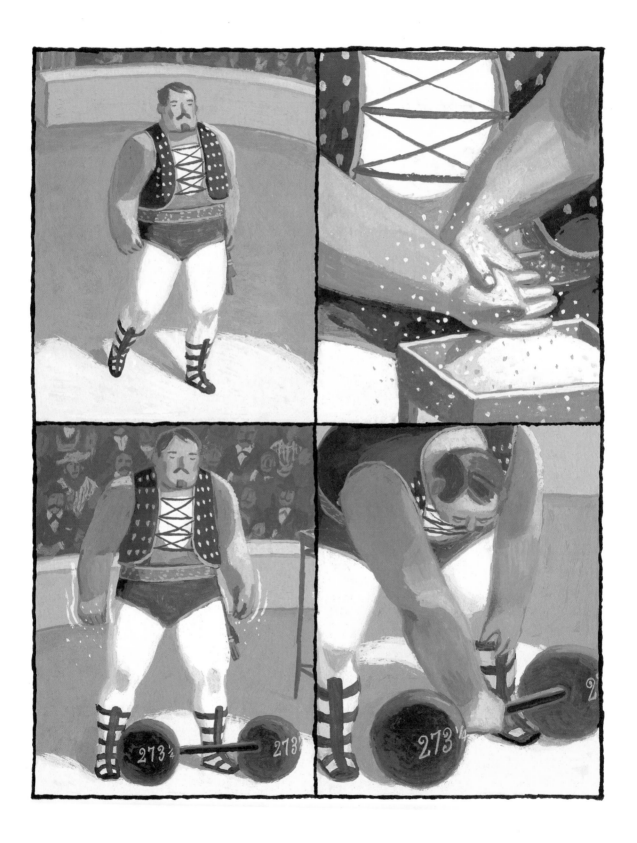

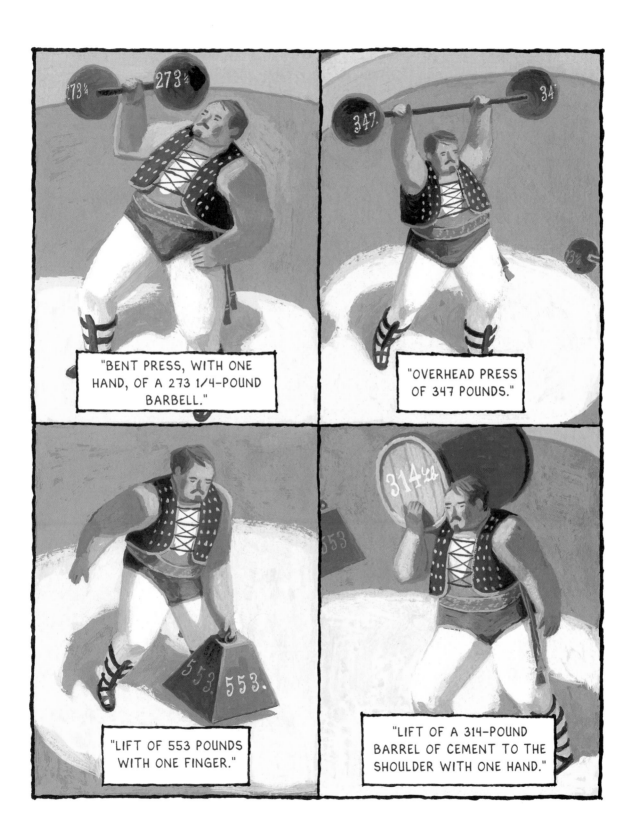

"BENT PRESS, WITH ONE HAND, OF A 273 1/4-POUND BARBELL."

"OVERHEAD PRESS OF 347 POUNDS."

"LIFT OF 553 POUNDS WITH ONE FINGER."

"LIFT OF A 314-POUND BARREL OF CEMENT TO THE SHOULDER WITH ONE HAND."

22

NOW, MAY I ASK EIGHTEEN OF THE HEAVIEST GENTLEMEN IN THE AUDIENCE TO KINDLY STEP UP ONTO THIS PLATFORM...

"BACK LIFT OF EIGHTEEN MEN, ESTIMATED WEIGHT 4,300 POUNDS."

AFTERWORD

By the end of the nineteenth century, weightlifting ranked among the most popular entertainments in the Western world. Part actors, part athletes (weightlifting was featured in the first modern Olympic Games in 1896), strongmen inspired awe and respect from their audiences.

Louis Cyr (1863-1912) was famous for his feats around the world. Like many strongmen of his day, he came from the province of Québec. Born in the small town of Saint-Cyprien de Napierville, he proved himself to be an extraordinary athlete from an early age and remained undefeated throughout his career. His skill is all the more impressive because he executed his lifts in slow, almost continuous movements, with no bending of the knees or jerking to assist him.

In those days strongmen's feats were frequently exaggerated by the newspapers. Many showmen changed their names to those of mythological or Biblical heroes such as Atlas, Hercules or Samson, encouraging people to think of them as superhuman. Some even used tricks to appear stronger and more impressive than they really were. One of Louis Cyr's rivals would fill barbells with sand, which was emptied through small holes into concealed buckets just before he lifted them.

Louis Cyr toured North America with large companies such as the John Robinson Circus and the Ringling Brothers before founding his own circus, which included thirty-five performers. He was the chief attraction but there were also equilibrists, clowns, other strongmen, jugglers, acrobats and more. Some of the performers in the Louis Cyr Circus are shown on the endpapers of this book.

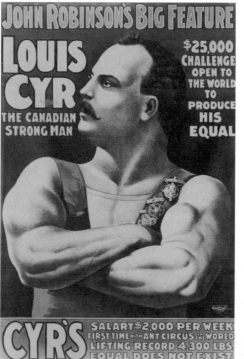

Most early circuses had sideshows or "freak" shows that featured people who were extraordinary in some way. They might be extremely short or tall or overweight, for example. These shows might also include fire-eaters or sword-swallowers. Sideshows were popular, in part, because they satisfied people's curiosity about the world. Circus owners were quick to turn this to their advantage, often cruelly exploiting performers who were physically challenged (although some may have preferred to have been part of a traveling circus, earning a living, rather than staying at home). But with advances in science and the ability to explain abnormalities, interest in sideshows at the circus gradually died out.

Louis Cyr eventually became so ill that he had to stop performing in his circus. Remarkably, despite dramatic improvements in strength training and lifting techniques, some of his records remain unequalled to this day.

A poster for the John Robinson Circus features its star attraction (facing page).

Louis Cyr poses for a formal photograph with his wife, Mélina, and their daughter, Émiliana (right).

The strongman is shown here, in 1896, ready to perform (bottom).

LOUIS CYR,
POLICE GAZETTE CHAMPION HEAVY LIFTER
OF THE WORLD.
CHAMPAGNE'S STUDIO, No. 8 HURD ST., LOWELL, MASS.

LOUIS CYR,
"Police Gazette" Champion Heavy Lifter of the World.

FOR FURTHER INFORMATION

Books

The Strongest Man in History: Louis Cyr by Ben Weider. Vancouver: Mitchell Press Ltd., 1976
A biography of Louis Cyr for older readers.

Circus by Linda Granfield. Toronto: Groundwood Books / Douglas & McIntyre Ltd., 1997
A comprehensive history of the circus for young readers.

Musée-halte Louis Cyr

This museum, in Saint-Jean-de-Matha, Québec, exhibits a number of artifacts that belonged to the strongman.

AUTHOR'S NOTE

The author gives special thanks to Ben Weider for his invaluable biography of Louis Cyr, and to Sylvie Ménard and the team at L'Université du Québec à Montréal, Service des archives et de gestion des documents, for their time and help in the research of this book. Other helpful resources were the Musée-halte Louis Cyr and *Les memoires de Louis Cyr, l'homme le plus fort du monde* by Septime Laferrière (Montreal: La Presse, 1908).

PICTURE CREDITS

The photographs on pages 26-27 are courtesy of L'Université du Québec à Montréal, Service des archives et de gestion des documents, Fonds d'archives Louis Cyr: 26 Copyright 1898, Courier Litho Co., Buffalo, N.Y., 120P-625:F3/1; 27 (top) 120P-035:F3/6; (bottom) 120P-625:F3/2.4.

STISKNE...
the American He...

...**N,**
...e Juggler

***Magdor RHINEHART*,**
Grand Ambassador
of the Kingdom of Lilliput

BENNATTI,
the Prince of Contortionists
from the Old World